First Facts®

easy origami

EASY OCEAN Origami

by Christopher L. Harbo

CAPSTONE PRESS
a capstone imprint

First Facts is published by Capstone Press,
1710 Roe Crest Drive, North Mankato, Minnesota 56003.
www.capstonepub.com

Books published by Capstone Press are manufactured with paper
containing at least 10 percent post-consumer waste.

Library of Congress Cataloging-in-Publication Data
Harbo, Christopher L.
 Easy ocean origami / by Christopher L. Harbo.
    p. cm.—(First facts. Easy origami)
 Includes bibliographical references.
 Summary: "Provides instructions and photo-illustrated diagrams for making a variety of easy
water-related origami models"—Provided by publisher.
 ISBN 978-1-4296-5385-5 (library binding)
 1. Origami—Juvenile literature. 2. Sea in art—Juvenile literature. I. Title. II. Series.

TT870.H322 2011
736'.982—dc22   2010024786

Editorial Credits
Designer: ALISON THIELE
Photo Studio Specialist: SARAH SCHUETTE
Scheduler: MARCY MORIN
Production Specialist: LAURA MANTHE

Photo Credits
Capstone Studio/Karon Dubke, all photos

Artistic Effects
Shutterstock/Klara Viskova, s26, Seamartini Graphics, SFerdon,
    stocksock, Z-art

ABOUT THE AUTHOR

Christopher L. Harbo loves origami. He began folding
paper several years ago and hasn't quit since. In
addition to decorative origami, he also enjoys folding
paper airplanes. When he's not practicing origami,
Christopher spends his free time reading Japanese
comic books and watching movies.

Printed in the United States of America in North Mankato, Minnesota.
112011   006456R

TABLE OF Contents

ORIGAMI Ocean

Dive into an origami ocean! This book is overflowing with seven simple models that have to do with water. Launch a paper ship that really floats. Make a windsurfer that glides with a puff of air. Fold a water lily that blooms in two colors. Don't worry if you've never folded paper before. Now is a great time to test the waters!

MATERIALS

Origami is a simple art that doesn't use many materials. You'll only need the following things to complete the projects in this book:

Origami Paper: Square origami paper comes in many fun colors and sizes. You can buy this paper in most craft stores.

Clear Tape: Most origami models don't need tape. But when they do, you'll be glad you have it handy.

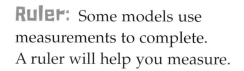

Ruler: Some models use measurements to complete. A ruler will help you measure.

Scissors: Sometimes a model needs a snip here or there to complete. Keep a scissors nearby.

Pencil: Use a pencil when you need to mark spots you measure with the ruler.

Craft Supplies: Markers and other craft supplies will help you decorate your models.

FOLDING TECHNIQUES

Folding paper is easier when you understand basic origami folds and symbols. Practice the folds on this list before trying the models in this book. Turn back to this list if you get stuck on a tricky step, or ask an adult for help.

Valley Folds are represented by a dashed line. One side of the paper is folded against the other like a book. A sharp fold is made by running your finger along the fold line.

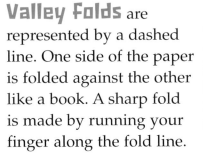
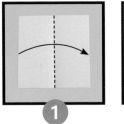

Mountain Folds are represented by a pink or white dashed and dotted line. The paper is folded sharply behind the model.

Squash Folds are formed by lifting one edge of a pocket. The pocket gets folded again so the spine gets flattened. The existing fold lines become new edges.

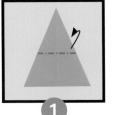

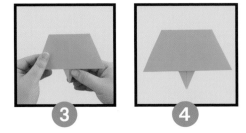

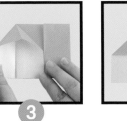

Inside reverse Folds are made by opening a pocket slightly. Then you fold the model inside itself along existing fold lines.

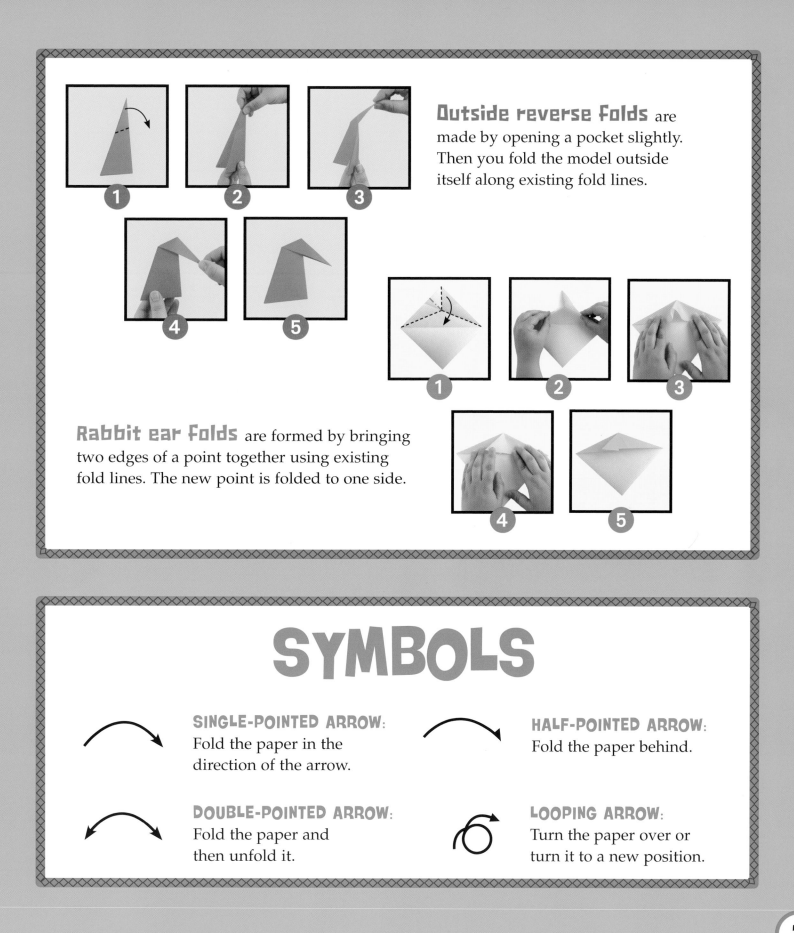

Outside reverse folds are made by opening a pocket slightly. Then you fold the model outside itself along existing fold lines.

Rabbit ear folds are formed by bringing two edges of a point together using existing fold lines. The new point is folded to one side.

SYMBOLS

SINGLE-POINTED ARROW:
Fold the paper in the direction of the arrow.

HALF-POINTED ARROW:
Fold the paper behind.

DOUBLE-POINTED ARROW:
Fold the paper and then unfold it.

LOOPING ARROW:
Turn the paper over or turn it to a new position.

ROYAL Yacht

Put on your captain's cap and raise a sail! Then imagine speeding across the ocean in this sharp paper yacht.

1

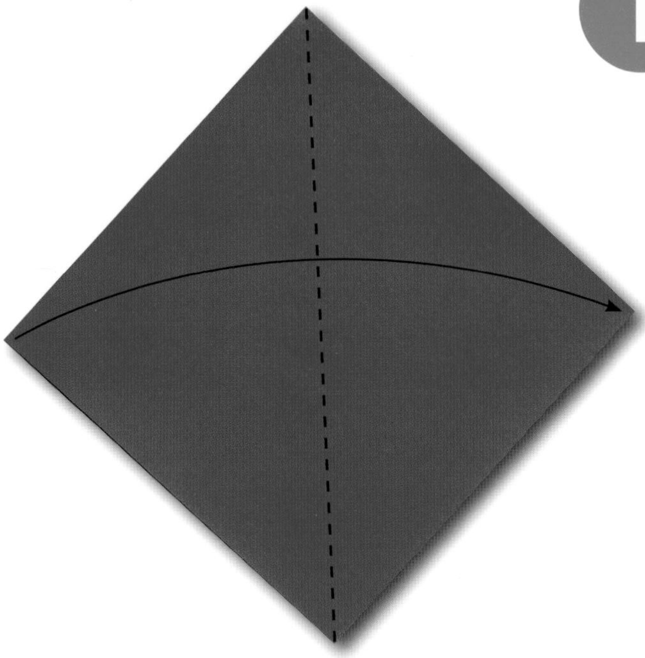

Start with the colored side of the paper face up. Valley fold the left point to the right point.

2

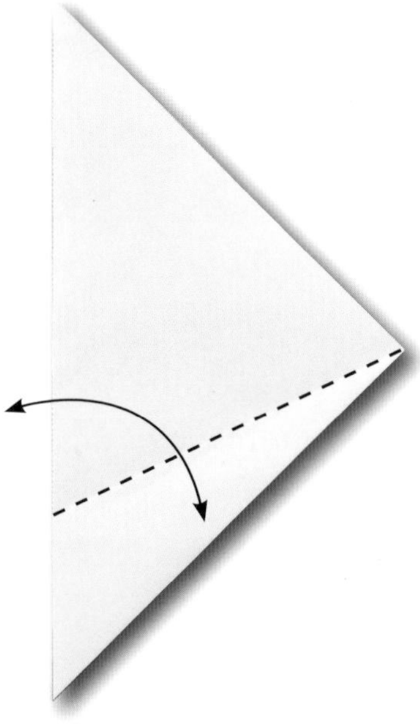

Valley fold the bottom point up and to the left. Note how one end of the fold meets the middle point of the triangle. Make a sharp fold and unfold.

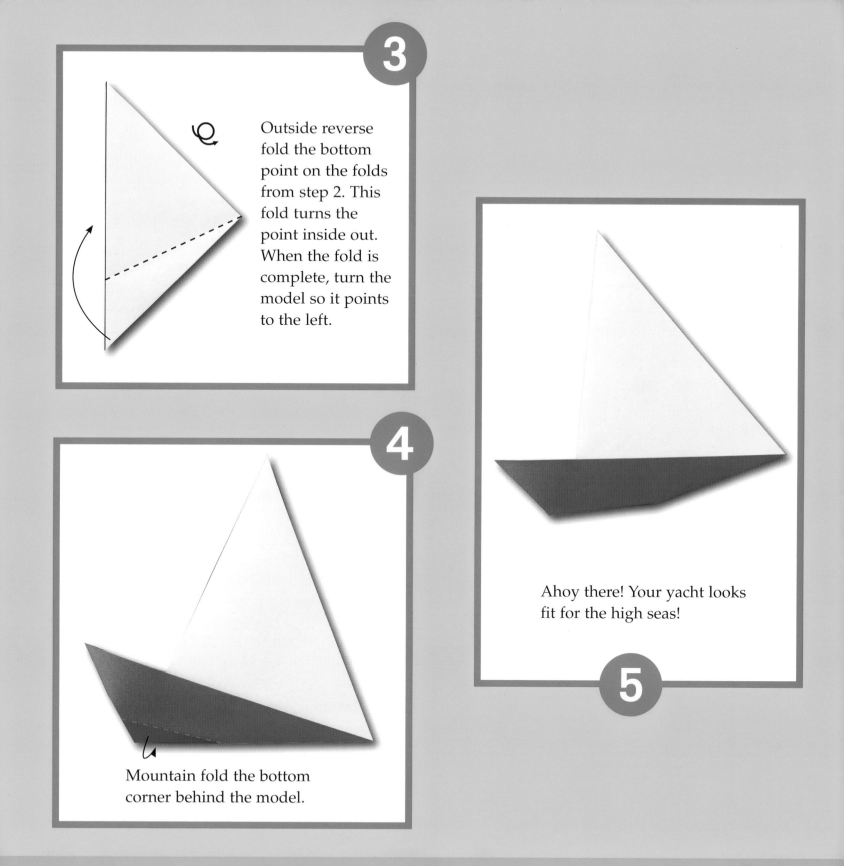

3

Outside reverse fold the bottom point on the folds from step 2. This fold turns the point inside out. When the fold is complete, turn the model so it points to the left.

4

Mountain fold the bottom corner behind the model.

5

Ahoy there! Your yacht looks fit for the high seas!

SECRET Tip Use markers or crayons to give your yacht's sail its own style.

FLOATING Ship

Traditional Model

Here's a paper ship that really floats! Fold a fleet of ships and set sail on an adventure.

1

Start with the colored side of the paper face down. Valley fold the bottom-left point to the top-right point.

2

Valley fold the bottom point past the top edge. Note how this fold slants slightly from right to left. Make a sharp fold and unfold.

3

Inside reverse fold the bottom point on the folds from step 2. This fold allows the point to swing up inside the model.

4

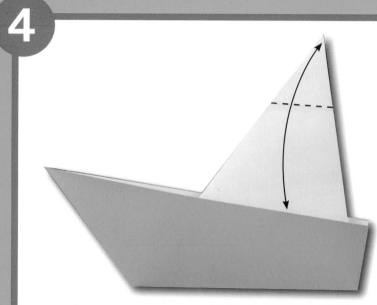

Valley fold the top point to the edge of the top layer. Make a sharp fold and unfold.

5

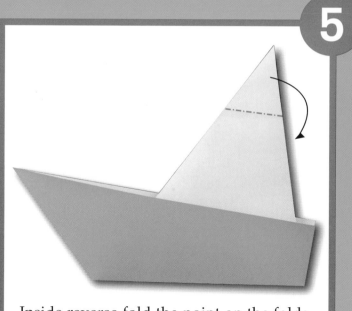

Inside reverse fold the point on the folds from step 4. This fold allows the top point to swing down inside the model.

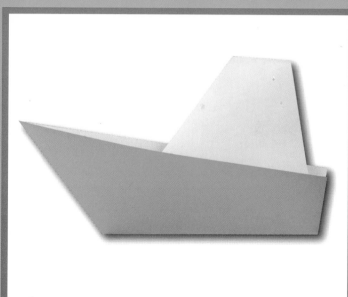

Float your ship in a pond or a kitchen sink.

6

SECRET Tip

Color both sides of your ship's bottom edges with a crayon. The crayon wax will protect the edges in the water. Your ship will float longer!

COOL Windsurfer

Traditional Model

Now you can go windsurfing without ever getting wet! Use a little lung power to send this tiny windsurfer scooting across a table.

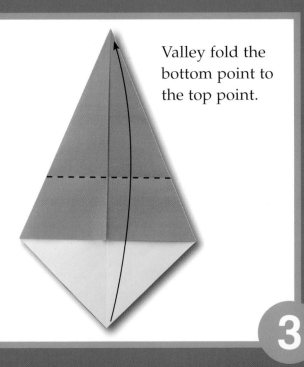

1

Start with the colored side of the paper face down. Valley fold the left point to the right point and unfold.

2

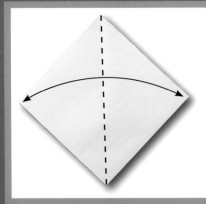

Valley fold the top-left edge to the center fold. Valley fold the top-right edge to the center fold.

3

Valley fold the bottom point to the top point.

4

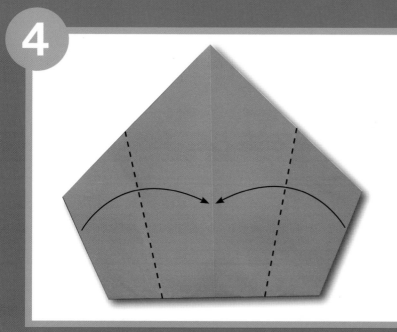

Valley fold the left and right edges to the center fold.

5

Lift the top layer. Valley fold its point past the bottom edge. This fold connects the slanted edges near the bottom of the model. Make a sharp fold and unfold the point halfway.

Blow on the back of the windsurfer's sail to see it glide.

6

 **SECRET Tip** Make windsurfers for all of your friends. Then hold races to see whose windsurfer is the fastest.

 13

BLUE Whale

Traditional Model

No animal on Earth is larger than the blue whale.
Find the biggest square of blue paper you can.
Then fold this gentle giant for your origami ocean.

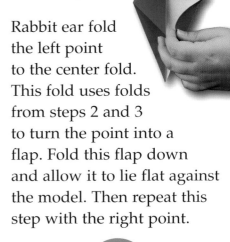

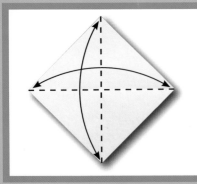

1 Start with the colored side of the paper face down. Valley fold the left point to the right point and unfold. Valley fold the top point to the bottom point and unfold.

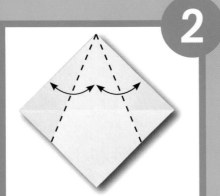

2 Valley fold the top-left edge to the center fold and unfold. Valley fold the top-right edge to the center fold and unfold.

3 Valley fold the bottom-left edge to the center fold and unfold. Valley fold the bottom-right edge to the center fold and unfold.

4 Rabbit ear fold the left point to the center fold. This fold uses folds from steps 2 and 3 to turn the point into a flap. Fold this flap down and allow it to lie flat against the model. Then repeat this step with the right point.

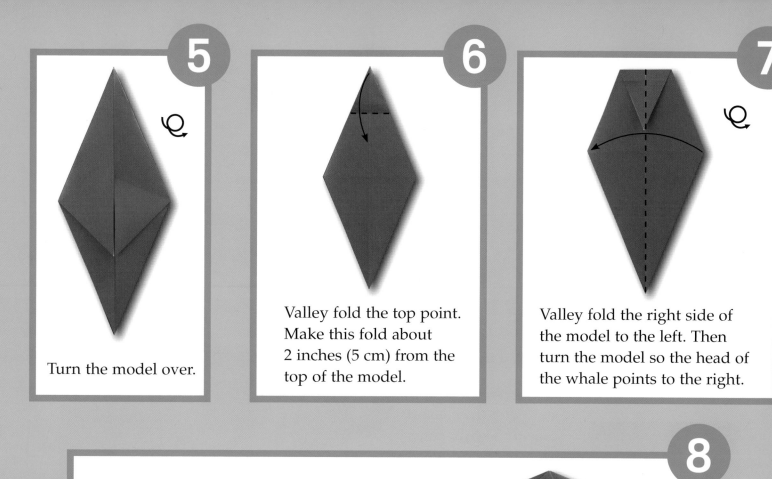

5

Turn the model over.

6

Valley fold the top point. Make this fold about 2 inches (5 cm) from the top of the model.

7

Valley fold the right side of the model to the left. Then turn the model so the head of the whale points to the right.

8

Valley fold the left point. Make this fold slant from left to right so the point sticks straight up. Make a sharp fold and unfold.

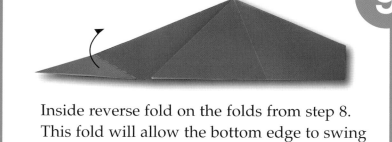

9

Inside reverse fold on the folds from step 8. This fold will allow the bottom edge to swing inside the model to make a tail.

10

Draw an underwater scene for your whale.

SECRET Tip Tuck a rolled piece of tape inside your whale's body. The tape will hold the two sides of the body together tightly.

CLEVER Sailboat

Traditional Model

Set sail on an origami adventure! This clever sailboat uses both sides of the paper to make two white sails and a colored hull.

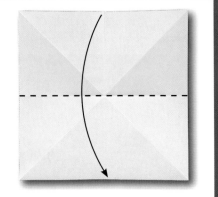

1 Start with the colored side of the paper face up. Valley fold the bottom-left corner to the top-right corner and unfold. Valley fold the top-left corner to the bottom-right corner and unfold.

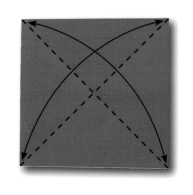

2 Turn the paper over.

3 Valley fold the left edge to the right edge and unfold.

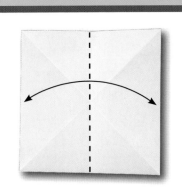

4 Valley fold the top edge to the bottom edge.

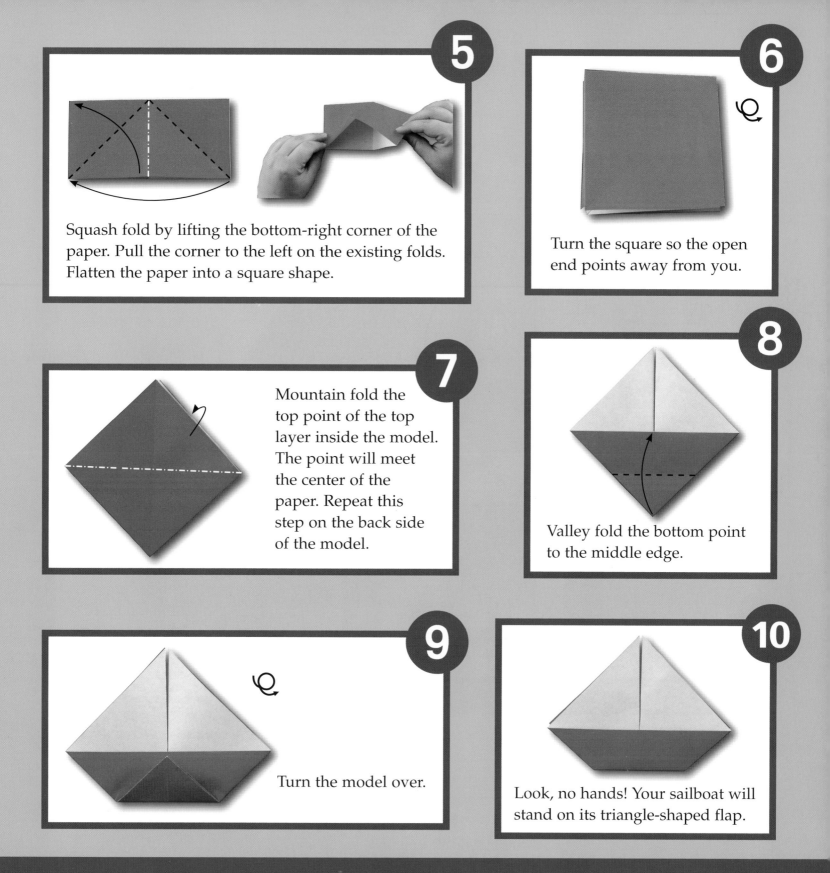

5

Squash fold by lifting the bottom-right corner of the paper. Pull the corner to the left on the existing folds. Flatten the paper into a square shape.

6

Turn the square so the open end points away from you.

7

Mountain fold the top point of the top layer inside the model. The point will meet the center of the paper. Repeat this step on the back side of the model.

8

Valley fold the bottom point to the middle edge.

9

Turn the model over.

10

Look, no hands! Your sailboat will stand on its triangle-shaped flap.

SECRET Tip

To make one sail shorter, mountain fold a sail behind the model. Then valley fold the sail back up. Make this fold a little below the mountain fold. Ta-da! You now have one short sail and one tall sail.

SWIMMING Goldfish

Traditional Model

Fold this model and surprise your friends with a snip, snip, snip. With three simple cuts, you'll turn a samurai helmet into a goldfish.

1

Start with the colored side of the paper face down. Valley fold the top point to the bottom point.

2

Valley fold the left and right points to the bottom point.

3

Lift the left side's top layer. Valley fold its bottom point to the top point. Repeat this step on the right side's top layer.

4

Lift the left side's top layer. Valley fold its top point past the outside edge. Note how the fold meets the center of the model. Repeat this step on the right side's top layer.

5

Valley fold the top layer of the bottom point. The point should rest about 1 inch (2.5 cm) from the top point.

6

Valley fold the edge made in step 5. The fold runs along the center edge of the model.

7

Mountain fold the bottom point behind the model.

8

Pull the top and bottom layers of the model apart. Flatten the model completely.

9

Use a scissors to cut along the top-right edge. The cut should end about .5 inch (1.3 cm) from the right corner. Then make similar cuts on both bottom-right edges.

10

Valley fold the right side's top layer. The fold will connect the ends of the cuts from step 9. Repeat this valley fold on the back side of the model.

11

Glub, glub, glub. Your goldfish is ready to swim.

SECRET Tip To make a samurai helmet, simply stop after step 7. Place the helmet on a doll's head or make one large enough for you to wear.

WATER Lily

Traditional Model

Real water lilies only bloom from June to September. But this paper water lily can brighten your day all year long.

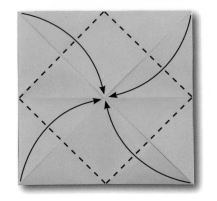

1 Start with the colored side of the large paper face down. Valley fold the left point to the right point and unfold. Valley fold the top point to the bottom point and unfold.

2 Valley fold all four points to the center.

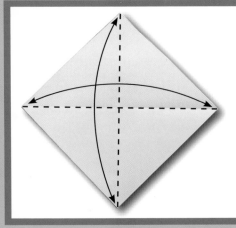

3 Valley fold all four corners to the center.

SPECIAL Note

This model uses two pieces of paper. One piece should be a 9.75-inch (25-cm) square. The other piece should be a 6-inch (15-cm) square.

4 Turn the model over.

5 Valley fold all four points to the center.

6 Valley fold all four inside points past the outside edges. Each fold should be about .25 inch (.64 cm) from the edge.

7 Turn the model over.

8 Lift the four inside points that make up the first layer of the model. Valley fold these points in half and unfold them slightly.

9 Lift the four inside corners that make up the second layer of the model. Valley fold these corners in half and unfold them slightly.

10 Repeat steps 1 through 9 with the small square.

11 Place the bottom corners of the small blossom into the center of the larger blossom.

12 Your water lily is blooming!

Origami
OCEAN FUN

READ More

Boonyadhistarn, Thiranut. *Origami: The Fun and Funky Art of Paper Folding.* Crafts. Mankato, Minn.: Capstone Press, 2007.

Boursin, Didier. *Folding for Fun.* Richmond Hill, Ont.: Firefly Books, 2007.

Engel, Peter. *10-Fold Origami: Fabulous Paperfolds You Can Make in 10 Steps or Less.* New York: Sterling Pub. Co. Inc., 2008.

Meinking, Mary. *Easy Origami.* Origami. Mankato, Minn.: Capstone Press, 2009.

INTERNET Sites

FactHound offers a safe, fun way to find Internet sites related to this book. All of the sites on FactHound have been researched by our staff.

Here's all you do:

Visit *www.facthound.com*

Type in this code: 9781429653855

Check out projects, games and lots more at
www.capstonekids.com

DATE DUE 11/13
not on
Rotation

DISCARDED

PRINTED IN U.S.A.